50 Pressure Cooking Game Recipes for Home

By: Kelly Johnson

Table of Contents

- Beef and Vegetable Stew
- Pasta Primavera
- Balsamic Chicken Thighs
- Chana Masala
- Curry Lentils
- Zucchini Fritters
- Apple Crisp
- Salmon with Dill Sauce
- Beef Bourguignon
- Pork Fried Rice
- Chicken Pho
- Ratatouille Pasta
- Lemon Garlic Potatoes
- Pesto Chicken Pasta
- Flan

Beef Stroganoff

Ingredients:

- 1 lb beef (sirloin or tenderloin), thinly sliced
- 1 onion, chopped
- 2 cups mushrooms, sliced
- 2 cups beef broth
- 1 cup sour cream
- 2 tbsp flour
- 2 tbsp butter
- Salt and pepper to taste
- Egg noodles or rice, for serving

Instructions:

1. In a skillet, melt butter over medium heat. Sauté onions until translucent.
2. Add mushrooms and cook until tender.
3. Add beef, cooking until browned. Season with salt and pepper.
4. Sprinkle flour over the beef and stir, then gradually add beef broth. Simmer for 10 minutes.
5. Stir in sour cream and heat through (do not boil).
6. Serve over cooked egg noodles or rice.

Delve into this comforting dish!

Chicken Tikka Masala

Ingredients:

- 1 lb chicken breast, cut into bite-sized pieces
- 1 cup plain yogurt
- 2 tbsp lemon juice
- 2 tbsp garam masala
- 1 tsp cumin
- 1 tsp paprika
- 1 tsp turmeric
- 2 tbsp vegetable oil
- 1 onion, chopped
- 2 cloves garlic, minced
- 1 inch ginger, grated
- 1 can (14 oz) crushed tomatoes
- 1 cup heavy cream
- Salt and pepper to taste
- Fresh cilantro, for garnish
- Cooked rice, for serving

Instructions:

1. In a bowl, mix yogurt, lemon juice, garam masala, cumin, paprika, and turmeric. Add chicken, coat well, and marinate for at least 1 hour (or overnight).
2. Heat oil in a skillet over medium heat. Sauté onions until golden. Add garlic and ginger, cooking until fragrant.
3. Add marinated chicken and cook until browned. Stir in crushed tomatoes and simmer for 10 minutes.
4. Add heavy cream, salt, and pepper. Simmer for another 5 minutes.
5. Garnish with cilantro and serve with rice.

Lentil Soup

Ingredients:

- 1 cup lentils (green or brown), rinsed
- 1 onion, chopped
- 2 carrots, diced
- 2 celery stalks, diced
- 3 cloves garlic, minced
- 6 cups vegetable broth
- 1 can (14 oz) diced tomatoes
- 1 tsp cumin
- 1 tsp thyme
- Salt and pepper to taste
- 2 tbsp olive oil
- Fresh parsley, for garnish

Instructions:

1. In a large pot, heat olive oil over medium heat. Sauté onions, carrots, and celery until softened.
2. Add garlic and cook for another minute.
3. Stir in lentils, broth, diced tomatoes, cumin, thyme, salt, and pepper.
4. Bring to a boil, then reduce heat and simmer for 30-35 minutes, until lentils are tender.
5. Garnish with fresh parsley before serving.

Garlic Mashed Potatoes

Ingredients:

- 2 lbs potatoes, peeled and cubed
- 4 cloves garlic, peeled
- 1/2 cup milk (or cream)
- 1/4 cup butter
- Salt and pepper to taste
- Fresh chives, for garnish (optional)

Instructions:

1. In a large pot, add potatoes and garlic, cover with water, and bring to a boil. Cook until potatoes are tender, about 15-20 minutes.
2. Drain and return potatoes and garlic to the pot. Add milk and butter.
3. Mash until smooth and creamy. Season with salt and pepper.
4. Garnish with fresh chives if desired, and serve warm.

Enjoy these delicious dishes!

Pulled Pork Tacos

Ingredients:

- 2 lbs pork shoulder
- 1 onion, chopped
- 3 cloves garlic, minced
- 1 cup BBQ sauce
- 1 tsp cumin
- 1 tsp paprika
- Salt and pepper to taste
- Corn or flour tortillas
- Toppings: diced onions, cilantro, lime wedges

Instructions:

1. Rub pork with cumin, paprika, salt, and pepper. Place in a slow cooker with onions and garlic.
2. Pour BBQ sauce over the pork. Cook on low for 8 hours or until tender.
3. Shred the pork with two forks. Serve in tortillas with toppings.

Quinoa and Black Bean Chili

Ingredients:

- 1 cup quinoa, rinsed
- 1 can (15 oz) black beans, drained
- 1 can (14 oz) diced tomatoes
- 1 onion, chopped
- 1 bell pepper, diced
- 2 cloves garlic, minced
- 2 cups vegetable broth
- 1 tbsp chili powder
- 1 tsp cumin
- Salt and pepper to taste
- Fresh cilantro, for garnish

Instructions:

1. In a pot, sauté onion, bell pepper, and garlic until softened.
2. Add quinoa, black beans, diced tomatoes, broth, chili powder, cumin, salt, and pepper.
3. Bring to a boil, then reduce heat and simmer for 20 minutes, until quinoa is cooked.
4. Garnish with fresh cilantro before serving.

Risotto with Mushrooms

Ingredients:

- 1 cup Arborio rice
- 4 cups vegetable broth
- 1 cup mushrooms, sliced
- 1 onion, chopped
- 2 cloves garlic, minced
- 1/2 cup white wine (optional)
- 1/2 cup grated Parmesan cheese
- 2 tbsp butter
- Salt and pepper to taste
- Fresh parsley, for garnish

Instructions:

1. In a saucepan, heat broth and keep warm.
2. In a large skillet, melt butter. Sauté onion and garlic until translucent, then add mushrooms.
3. Stir in Arborio rice and cook for 1-2 minutes. Add wine (if using) and let it absorb.
4. Gradually add warm broth, one ladle at a time, stirring frequently until absorbed. Repeat until rice is creamy and al dente.
5. Stir in Parmesan, salt, and pepper. Garnish with parsley before serving.

Shrimp Etouffee

Ingredients:

- 1 lb shrimp, peeled and deveined
- 1 onion, chopped
- 1 bell pepper, diced
- 2 celery stalks, diced
- 3 cloves garlic, minced
- 1/4 cup flour
- 3 cups seafood or chicken broth
- 1 tbsp Cajun seasoning
- 2 tbsp vegetable oil
- Salt and pepper to taste
- Cooked rice, for serving
- Green onions, for garnish

Instructions:

1. In a large pot, heat oil and make a roux with flour, cooking until golden brown.
2. Add onion, bell pepper, celery, and garlic; cook until softened.
3. Stir in broth, Cajun seasoning, salt, and pepper. Simmer for 15 minutes.
4. Add shrimp and cook until pink. Serve over rice, garnished with green onions.

Beef and Broccoli

Ingredients:

- 1 lb beef (flank or sirloin), sliced thinly
- 2 cups broccoli florets
- 1/4 cup soy sauce
- 2 tbsp oyster sauce
- 2 cloves garlic, minced
- 1 tbsp cornstarch
- 2 tbsp vegetable oil
- Cooked rice, for serving

Instructions:

1. In a bowl, mix soy sauce, oyster sauce, garlic, and cornstarch. Add beef and marinate for 30 minutes.
2. In a skillet, heat oil over high heat. Add beef and cook until browned. Remove and set aside.
3. In the same skillet, add broccoli and a splash of water. Cook until tender.
4. Return beef to the skillet, stirring to combine. Serve over cooked rice.

Moroccan Chickpea Stew

Ingredients:

- 1 can (15 oz) chickpeas, drained
- 1 onion, chopped
- 2 carrots, diced
- 1 bell pepper, diced
- 1 can (14 oz) diced tomatoes
- 1 cup vegetable broth
- 1 tbsp cumin
- 1 tbsp paprika
- 1 tsp cinnamon
- Salt and pepper to taste
- 2 tbsp olive oil
- Fresh cilantro, for garnish

Instructions:

1. In a pot, heat olive oil and sauté onion, carrots, and bell pepper until softened.
2. Add chickpeas, diced tomatoes, broth, cumin, paprika, cinnamon, salt, and pepper.
3. Bring to a boil, then reduce heat and simmer for 20-25 minutes.
4. Garnish with fresh cilantro before serving.

Creamy Tomato Basil Soup

Ingredients:

- 2 cans (14 oz) diced tomatoes
- 1 onion, chopped
- 2 cloves garlic, minced
- 1 cup vegetable broth
- 1/2 cup heavy cream
- 1/4 cup fresh basil, chopped
- Salt and pepper to taste
- 2 tbsp olive oil

Instructions:

1. In a pot, heat olive oil and sauté onion and garlic until softened.
2. Add diced tomatoes and broth; bring to a simmer for 15 minutes.
3. Blend until smooth, then stir in heavy cream, basil, salt, and pepper.
4. Heat through and serve warm.

Enjoy these delicious dishes!

Spaghetti and Meatballs

Ingredients:

- 1 lb ground beef
- 1/2 cup breadcrumbs
- 1/4 cup grated Parmesan cheese
- 1 egg
- 2 cloves garlic, minced
- 1 tsp Italian seasoning
- Salt and pepper to taste
- 2 cups marinara sauce
- 12 oz spaghetti
- Fresh basil, for garnish

Instructions:

1. In a bowl, combine ground beef, breadcrumbs, Parmesan, egg, garlic, Italian seasoning, salt, and pepper. Form into meatballs.
2. In a skillet, brown meatballs on all sides. Add marinara sauce and simmer for 20 minutes.
3. Cook spaghetti according to package instructions. Serve meatballs over spaghetti, garnished with fresh basil.

Barbecue Ribs

Ingredients:

- 2 lbs pork ribs
- 1 cup BBQ sauce
- 1 tbsp paprika
- 1 tbsp garlic powder
- 1 tbsp onion powder
- Salt and pepper to taste

Instructions:

1. Preheat oven to 300°F (150°C). Season ribs with paprika, garlic powder, onion powder, salt, and pepper.
2. Place ribs on a baking sheet and cover with foil. Bake for 2.5 to 3 hours until tender.
3. Remove foil, brush with BBQ sauce, and broil for 5-10 minutes until caramelized.

Coconut Curry Chicken

Ingredients:

- 1 lb chicken breast, cubed
- 1 can (14 oz) coconut milk
- 2 tbsp red curry paste
- 1 onion, chopped
- 2 cloves garlic, minced
- 1 inch ginger, grated
- 2 cups vegetables (bell pepper, zucchini, etc.)
- Salt to taste
- Fresh cilantro, for garnish
- Cooked rice, for serving

Instructions:

1. In a pot, sauté onion, garlic, and ginger until fragrant. Add chicken and cook until browned.
2. Stir in curry paste and cook for 1 minute. Add coconut milk and vegetables, simmer for 15-20 minutes.
3. Season with salt and serve over rice, garnished with cilantro.

Jambalaya

Ingredients:

- 1 lb chicken breast, diced
- 1 lb shrimp, peeled and deveined
- 1 sausage (Andouille or smoked), sliced
- 1 onion, chopped
- 1 bell pepper, diced
- 2 celery stalks, diced
- 3 cloves garlic, minced
- 1 can (14 oz) diced tomatoes
- 2 cups chicken broth
- 1 tbsp Cajun seasoning
- 1 1/2 cups rice
- Salt and pepper to taste

Instructions:

1. In a large pot, sauté onion, bell pepper, and celery until softened. Add garlic and cook for another minute.
2. Stir in chicken and sausage, cooking until browned. Add diced tomatoes, broth, Cajun seasoning, rice, salt, and pepper.
3. Bring to a boil, then reduce heat and simmer for 20-25 minutes until rice is cooked. Add shrimp in the last 5 minutes of cooking.

Sweet Potato Casserole

Ingredients:

- 4 cups mashed sweet potatoes (about 4 large)
- 1/2 cup brown sugar
- 1/4 cup butter, melted
- 1/4 cup milk
- 1 tsp vanilla extract
- 1/2 tsp cinnamon
- 1 cup mini marshmallows (optional)

Instructions:

1. Preheat oven to 350°F (175°C). In a bowl, mix sweet potatoes, brown sugar, butter, milk, vanilla, and cinnamon until smooth.
2. Spread mixture in a baking dish. Top with marshmallows if desired.
3. Bake for 25-30 minutes until heated through and marshmallows are golden.

Chicken and Rice

Ingredients:

- 1 lb chicken thighs or breasts, diced
- 1 onion, chopped
- 2 cloves garlic, minced
- 1 cup long-grain rice
- 2 cups chicken broth
- 1 tsp paprika
- Salt and pepper to taste
- 2 tbsp olive oil
- Fresh parsley, for garnish

Instructions:

1. In a pot, heat olive oil and sauté onion and garlic until softened. Add chicken and cook until browned.
2. Stir in rice, broth, paprika, salt, and pepper. Bring to a boil, then reduce heat, cover, and simmer for 20 minutes.
3. Fluff with a fork and garnish with fresh parsley before serving.

Beef Chili

Ingredients:

- 1 lb ground beef
- 1 onion, chopped
- 2 cloves garlic, minced
- 1 can (15 oz) kidney beans, drained
- 1 can (15 oz) diced tomatoes
- 2 tbsp chili powder
- 1 tsp cumin
- Salt and pepper to taste
- 2 cups beef broth

Instructions:

1. In a pot, brown ground beef with onion and garlic. Drain excess fat.
2. Stir in kidney beans, diced tomatoes, chili powder, cumin, salt, pepper, and beef broth.
3. Simmer for 30 minutes. Serve hot, garnished with cheese or sour cream if desired.

Ratatouille

Ingredients:

- 1 eggplant, diced
- 1 zucchini, diced
- 1 bell pepper, diced
- 1 onion, chopped
- 2 cloves garlic, minced
- 1 can (14 oz) diced tomatoes
- 1 tsp thyme
- 1 tsp basil
- Salt and pepper to taste
- 2 tbsp olive oil

Instructions:

1. In a large skillet, heat olive oil and sauté onion and garlic until softened.
2. Add eggplant, zucchini, and bell pepper. Cook until tender.
3. Stir in diced tomatoes, thyme, basil, salt, and pepper. Simmer for 20 minutes. Serve warm.

Enjoy these flavorful dishes!

Stuffed Bell Peppers

Ingredients:

- 4 bell peppers, tops cut off and seeds removed
- 1 lb ground beef or turkey
- 1 cup cooked rice
- 1 can (14 oz) diced tomatoes
- 1 onion, chopped
- 2 cloves garlic, minced
- 1 tsp Italian seasoning
- Salt and pepper to taste
- 1 cup shredded cheese (optional)

Instructions:

1. Preheat oven to 375°F (190°C). In a skillet, sauté onion and garlic until softened. Add meat, cooking until browned.
2. Mix in rice, diced tomatoes, Italian seasoning, salt, and pepper.
3. Stuff mixture into bell peppers and place in a baking dish. Top with cheese if desired.
4. Bake for 30-35 minutes until peppers are tender.

Greek Lemon Chicken Soup

Ingredients:

- 1 lb chicken breast, cooked and shredded
- 6 cups chicken broth
- 1 cup orzo pasta
- 2 eggs
- 1/4 cup lemon juice
- 1 cup spinach, chopped
- Salt and pepper to taste
- Fresh dill, for garnish

Instructions:

1. In a pot, bring chicken broth to a boil. Add orzo and cook until tender.
2. In a bowl, whisk eggs and lemon juice. Slowly add a ladle of hot broth to temper the eggs.
3. Stir the egg mixture back into the pot, then add chicken and spinach. Season with salt and pepper.
4. Garnish with fresh dill before serving.

Vegetable Biryani

Ingredients:

- 1 1/2 cups basmati rice, rinsed
- 2 cups mixed vegetables (carrots, peas, beans)
- 1 onion, sliced
- 2 cloves garlic, minced
- 1 tbsp ginger, grated
- 2 cups vegetable broth
- 1 tbsp biryani masala or curry powder
- Salt and pepper to taste
- 2 tbsp oil
- Fresh cilantro, for garnish

Instructions:

1. In a pot, heat oil and sauté onion, garlic, and ginger until fragrant. Add mixed vegetables and cook for 5 minutes.
2. Stir in rice, broth, biryani masala, salt, and pepper. Bring to a boil.
3. Reduce heat, cover, and simmer for 15-20 minutes until rice is cooked. Fluff with a fork and garnish with cilantro.

Teriyaki Salmon

Ingredients:

- 4 salmon fillets
- 1/4 cup soy sauce
- 2 tbsp honey
- 1 tbsp rice vinegar
- 2 cloves garlic, minced
- 1 tbsp ginger, grated
- Sesame seeds and green onions for garnish

Instructions:

1. In a bowl, whisk together soy sauce, honey, rice vinegar, garlic, and ginger. Marinate salmon for 30 minutes.
2. Preheat oven to 400°F (200°C). Place salmon on a baking sheet and brush with marinade.
3. Bake for 12-15 minutes until cooked through. Garnish with sesame seeds and green onions.

Goulash

Ingredients:

- 1 lb ground beef
- 1 onion, chopped
- 2 cloves garlic, minced
- 1 can (15 oz) diced tomatoes
- 2 cups beef broth
- 2 cups elbow macaroni
- 1 tbsp paprika
- Salt and pepper to taste
- 1 cup shredded cheese (optional)

Instructions:

1. In a pot, brown ground beef with onion and garlic. Drain excess fat.
2. Stir in diced tomatoes, beef broth, macaroni, paprika, salt, and pepper. Bring to a boil.
3. Reduce heat and simmer until macaroni is cooked. Stir in cheese if desired before serving.

Split Pea Soup

Ingredients:

- 1 cup split peas, rinsed
- 1 onion, chopped
- 2 carrots, diced
- 2 celery stalks, diced
- 3 cloves garlic, minced
- 6 cups vegetable or chicken broth
- 1 bay leaf
- Salt and pepper to taste
- 2 tbsp olive oil

Instructions:

1. In a pot, heat olive oil and sauté onion, carrots, and celery until softened. Add garlic and cook for another minute.
2. Stir in split peas, broth, bay leaf, salt, and pepper. Bring to a boil.
3. Reduce heat and simmer for 45-60 minutes until peas are tender. Remove bay leaf and blend if desired.

Thai Peanut Chicken

Ingredients:

- 1 lb chicken breast, sliced
- 1/4 cup peanut butter
- 1/4 cup soy sauce
- 2 tbsp honey
- 2 cloves garlic, minced
- 1 tbsp ginger, grated
- 1 cup bell peppers, sliced
- Cooked rice, for serving
- Chopped peanuts and cilantro for garnish

Instructions:

1. In a bowl, whisk together peanut butter, soy sauce, honey, garlic, and ginger.
2. In a skillet, cook chicken until browned. Add bell peppers and cook for another 3-4 minutes.
3. Stir in the peanut sauce and cook until heated through. Serve over rice, garnished with peanuts and cilantro.

Eggplant Parmesan

Ingredients:

- 2 eggplants, sliced
- 2 cups marinara sauce
- 2 cups mozzarella cheese, shredded
- 1/2 cup grated Parmesan cheese
- 1 cup breadcrumbs
- 1 egg, beaten
- Olive oil for frying
- Fresh basil, for garnish

Instructions:

1. Preheat oven to 375°F (190°C). Salt eggplant slices and let sit for 30 minutes to draw out moisture. Rinse and pat dry.
2. Dip eggplant slices in egg, then breadcrumbs. Fry in olive oil until golden brown.
3. In a baking dish, layer marinara sauce, eggplant, mozzarella, and Parmesan. Repeat layers.
4. Bake for 25-30 minutes until bubbly. Garnish with fresh basil before serving.

Enjoy these delightful dishes!

Meatloaf

Ingredients:

- 1 1/2 lbs ground beef
- 1 cup breadcrumbs
- 1/2 cup milk
- 1/2 cup ketchup
- 1 onion, chopped
- 2 cloves garlic, minced
- 1 egg
- 1 tsp salt
- 1/2 tsp pepper
- 1 tsp Worcestershire sauce

Instructions:

1. Preheat oven to 350°F (175°C). In a bowl, mix all ingredients until well combined.
2. Shape mixture into a loaf and place in a baking dish. Top with extra ketchup if desired.
3. Bake for 1 hour until cooked through. Let rest before slicing.

Cranberry-Orange Glazed Ham

Ingredients:

- 1 fully cooked ham (5-7 lbs)
- 1 cup cranberry sauce
- 1/2 cup orange juice
- 1/4 cup brown sugar
- 1 tsp ground cinnamon

Instructions:

1. Preheat oven to 325°F (165°C). Place ham in a roasting pan.
2. In a bowl, mix cranberry sauce, orange juice, brown sugar, and cinnamon. Brush glaze over ham.
3. Cover with foil and bake for about 1.5 hours, basting every 30 minutes, until heated through.

Butternut Squash Soup

Ingredients:

- 1 butternut squash, peeled and cubed
- 1 onion, chopped
- 2 cloves garlic, minced
- 4 cups vegetable broth
- 1/2 cup cream (optional)
- Salt and pepper to taste
- 2 tbsp olive oil

Instructions:

1. In a pot, heat olive oil and sauté onion and garlic until softened. Add squash and broth.
2. Bring to a boil, then reduce heat and simmer until squash is tender, about 20 minutes.
3. Blend until smooth, stir in cream if desired, and season with salt and pepper.

Cabbage Rolls

Ingredients:

- 1 large head of cabbage
- 1 lb ground beef or turkey
- 1 cup rice, cooked
- 1 onion, chopped
- 1 can (15 oz) tomato sauce
- 1 egg
- Salt and pepper to taste

Instructions:

1. Preheat oven to 350°F (175°C). Boil cabbage leaves until tender, about 5 minutes.
2. In a bowl, mix meat, rice, onion, egg, salt, and pepper. Place filling in cabbage leaves and roll tightly.
3. Place rolls in a baking dish, cover with tomato sauce, and bake for 1 hour.

Chicken Enchiladas

Ingredients:

- 2 cups cooked chicken, shredded
- 1 cup cheese, shredded (cheddar or Monterey Jack)
- 1 can (10 oz) enchilada sauce
- 8 tortillas
- 1/2 onion, chopped
- 1 tsp cumin
- 1/2 tsp chili powder
- Fresh cilantro, for garnish

Instructions:

1. Preheat oven to 350°F (175°C). In a bowl, mix chicken, half the cheese, onion, cumin, and chili powder.
2. Fill tortillas with the mixture, roll up, and place seam-side down in a baking dish. Pour enchilada sauce over the top.
3. Sprinkle remaining cheese on top and bake for 20-25 minutes. Garnish with cilantro before serving.

Tomato Risotto

Ingredients:

- 1 cup Arborio rice
- 1 can (14 oz) diced tomatoes
- 1 onion, chopped
- 2 cloves garlic, minced
- 4 cups vegetable broth
- 1/2 cup Parmesan cheese, grated
- 2 tbsp olive oil
- Salt and pepper to taste
- Fresh basil, for garnish

Instructions:

1. In a saucepan, heat broth and keep warm. In a separate pot, heat olive oil and sauté onion and garlic until translucent.
2. Add Arborio rice and cook for 1-2 minutes. Stir in diced tomatoes and cook for another minute.
3. Gradually add warm broth, one ladle at a time, stirring frequently until absorbed. Stir in Parmesan, salt, and pepper. Garnish with basil.

BBQ Chicken

Ingredients:

- 4 chicken breasts
- 1 cup BBQ sauce
- Salt and pepper to taste
- Olive oil for grilling

Instructions:

1. Preheat grill to medium-high heat. Season chicken with salt and pepper.
2. Grill chicken for 6-7 minutes per side, brushing with BBQ sauce during the last few minutes of cooking.
3. Cook until internal temperature reaches 165°F (75°C). Serve with extra BBQ sauce.

Clam Chowder

Ingredients:

- 4 slices bacon, chopped
- 1 onion, chopped
- 2 cups potatoes, diced
- 2 cups clam juice
- 1 can (15 oz) clams, drained
- 1 cup heavy cream
- Salt and pepper to taste
- Fresh parsley, for garnish

Instructions:

1. In a pot, cook bacon until crispy. Remove and set aside, leaving drippings.
2. Sauté onion in bacon drippings until softened. Add potatoes and clam juice, bringing to a boil. Simmer until potatoes are tender.
3. Stir in clams, heavy cream, salt, and pepper. Heat through and garnish with bacon and parsley.

Enjoy these comforting dishes!

Beef and Vegetable Stew

Ingredients:

- 2 lbs beef chuck, cubed
- 4 cups beef broth
- 3 carrots, sliced
- 3 potatoes, diced
- 1 onion, chopped
- 2 cloves garlic, minced
- 2 tbsp tomato paste
- 1 tsp thyme
- Salt and pepper to taste
- 2 tbsp olive oil

Instructions:

1. In a large pot, heat olive oil over medium heat. Brown beef cubes, then remove and set aside.
2. In the same pot, sauté onion and garlic until softened. Stir in tomato paste, then add beef back in.
3. Add broth, carrots, potatoes, thyme, salt, and pepper. Bring to a boil, then reduce heat and simmer for 1.5-2 hours until beef is tender.

Pasta Primavera

Ingredients:

- 12 oz pasta (penne or fettuccine)
- 2 cups mixed vegetables (bell peppers, zucchini, carrots)
- 3 cloves garlic, minced
- 1/4 cup olive oil
- 1/2 cup Parmesan cheese, grated
- Salt and pepper to taste
- Fresh basil, for garnish

Instructions:

1. Cook pasta according to package instructions. Drain and set aside.
2. In a skillet, heat olive oil and sauté garlic until fragrant. Add vegetables and cook until tender.
3. Toss cooked pasta with vegetables, Parmesan, salt, and pepper. Garnish with fresh basil before serving.

Balsamic Chicken Thighs

Ingredients:

- 4 chicken thighs, bone-in and skin-on
- 1/2 cup balsamic vinegar
- 2 tbsp honey
- 2 cloves garlic, minced
- Salt and pepper to taste
- Fresh rosemary, for garnish

Instructions:

1. Preheat oven to 400°F (200°C). In a bowl, mix balsamic vinegar, honey, garlic, salt, and pepper.
2. Place chicken thighs in a baking dish and pour marinade over them. Bake for 35-40 minutes until cooked through.
3. Garnish with fresh rosemary before serving.

Chana Masala

Ingredients:

- 2 cans (15 oz each) chickpeas, drained
- 1 onion, chopped
- 2 tomatoes, diced
- 2 cloves garlic, minced
- 1 tbsp ginger, grated
- 1 tbsp cumin
- 1 tbsp coriander
- 1 tsp garam masala
- Salt to taste
- Fresh cilantro, for garnish

Instructions:

1. In a pot, sauté onion, garlic, and ginger until softened. Add tomatoes and cook until saucy.
2. Stir in chickpeas, cumin, coriander, garam masala, and salt. Simmer for 15-20 minutes.
3. Garnish with fresh cilantro before serving.

Curry Lentils

Ingredients:

- 1 cup lentils (red or green), rinsed
- 1 onion, chopped
- 2 cloves garlic, minced
- 1 tbsp curry powder
- 4 cups vegetable broth
- 1 can (14 oz) coconut milk
- Salt and pepper to taste
- Fresh cilantro, for garnish

Instructions:

1. In a pot, sauté onion and garlic until softened. Add curry powder and cook for 1 minute.
2. Stir in lentils, broth, and coconut milk. Bring to a boil, then reduce heat and simmer for 25-30 minutes until lentils are tender.
3. Season with salt and pepper, and garnish with cilantro before serving.

Zucchini Fritters

Ingredients:

- 2 medium zucchinis, grated
- 1/2 cup flour
- 1/4 cup grated Parmesan cheese
- 1 egg, beaten
- 2 green onions, chopped
- Salt and pepper to taste
- Olive oil for frying

Instructions:

1. Squeeze excess moisture from grated zucchini. In a bowl, mix zucchini, flour, Parmesan, egg, green onions, salt, and pepper.
2. Heat olive oil in a skillet. Drop spoonfuls of the mixture into the skillet and flatten slightly.
3. Fry until golden brown on both sides. Drain on paper towels before serving.

Apple Crisp

Ingredients:

- 4 cups sliced apples
- 1/2 cup brown sugar
- 1 tsp cinnamon
- 1/2 cup oats
- 1/2 cup flour
- 1/4 cup butter, melted
- Pinch of salt

Instructions:

1. Preheat oven to 350°F (175°C). In a bowl, toss apples with brown sugar and cinnamon. Place in a baking dish.
2. In another bowl, mix oats, flour, melted butter, and salt until crumbly. Sprinkle over apples.
3. Bake for 30-35 minutes until apples are tender and topping is golden brown.

Salmon with Dill Sauce

Ingredients:

- 4 salmon fillets
- 1/2 cup sour cream
- 2 tbsp fresh dill, chopped
- 1 tbsp lemon juice
- Salt and pepper to taste
- Olive oil for cooking

Instructions:

1. In a bowl, mix sour cream, dill, lemon juice, salt, and pepper. Set aside.
2. Heat olive oil in a skillet over medium-high heat. Cook salmon fillets skin-side down for 5-7 minutes, then flip and cook for another 3-4 minutes.
3. Serve salmon topped with dill sauce.

Enjoy these delicious recipes!

Beef Bourguignon

Ingredients:

- 2 lbs beef chuck, cut into cubes
- 4 cups red wine
- 2 cups beef broth
- 4 slices bacon, chopped
- 1 onion, chopped
- 2 carrots, sliced
- 2 cloves garlic, minced
- 2 tbsp tomato paste
- 1 bouquet garni (thyme, bay leaf, parsley)
- 1 lb mushrooms, quartered
- Salt and pepper to taste
- Olive oil for cooking

Instructions:

1. In a large pot, cook bacon until crispy. Remove and set aside, leaving drippings.
2. Brown beef cubes in the bacon fat. Remove and set aside.
3. Sauté onion and carrots in the pot, then add garlic and tomato paste. Stir in wine, broth, and bouquet garni.
4. Return beef and bacon to the pot. Simmer covered for 2-3 hours until tender. Add mushrooms in the last 30 minutes.

Pork Fried Rice

Ingredients:

- 2 cups cooked rice (preferably day-old)
- 1 lb pork tenderloin, diced
- 2 eggs, beaten
- 1 cup mixed vegetables (peas, carrots, corn)
- 3 green onions, sliced
- 3 tbsp soy sauce
- 2 tbsp sesame oil
- Salt and pepper to taste

Instructions:

1. In a skillet or wok, heat sesame oil. Cook pork until browned. Push to one side and scramble eggs on the other side.
2. Add mixed vegetables and cook until heated through. Stir in rice, soy sauce, green onions, salt, and pepper.
3. Stir-fry until everything is well combined and heated through.

Chicken Pho

Ingredients:

- 1 lb chicken breast
- 8 cups chicken broth
- 1 onion, halved
- 2 inches ginger, sliced
- 2 star anise
- 1 cinnamon stick
- 1 tbsp fish sauce
- Rice noodles
- Fresh basil, cilantro, lime, and sliced jalapeños for serving

Instructions:

1. In a pot, combine broth, onion, ginger, star anise, cinnamon, and fish sauce. Bring to a simmer.
2. Add chicken and cook until tender. Remove chicken, shred, and return to the pot.
3. Cook rice noodles according to package instructions. Serve soup over noodles, garnished with basil, cilantro, lime, and jalapeños.

Ratatouille Pasta

Ingredients:

- 8 oz pasta (penne or fusilli)
- 1 zucchini, diced
- 1 eggplant, diced
- 1 bell pepper, diced
- 1 onion, chopped
- 2 cloves garlic, minced
- 1 can (14 oz) diced tomatoes
- 1 tsp Italian seasoning
- Salt and pepper to taste
- Olive oil for cooking
- Fresh basil, for garnish

Instructions:

1. Cook pasta according to package instructions. Drain and set aside.
2. In a skillet, heat olive oil and sauté onion and garlic until fragrant. Add zucchini, eggplant, and bell pepper. Cook until tender.
3. Stir in diced tomatoes, Italian seasoning, salt, and pepper. Simmer for 10 minutes.
4. Toss pasta with the ratatouille mixture and garnish with fresh basil before serving.

Lemon Garlic Potatoes

Ingredients:

- 2 lbs baby potatoes, halved
- 4 cloves garlic, minced
- 1/4 cup olive oil
- Juice of 1 lemon
- 1 tsp dried oregano
- Salt and pepper to taste
- Fresh parsley, for garnish

Instructions:

1. Preheat oven to 400°F (200°C). In a bowl, combine potatoes, garlic, olive oil, lemon juice, oregano, salt, and pepper.
2. Spread potatoes on a baking sheet in a single layer. Roast for 30-35 minutes until golden and tender.
3. Garnish with fresh parsley before serving.

Pesto Chicken Pasta

Ingredients:

- 12 oz pasta (spaghetti or penne)
- 2 cups cooked chicken, shredded
- 1 cup pesto sauce
- 1/2 cup cherry tomatoes, halved
- 1/2 cup Parmesan cheese, grated
- Salt and pepper to taste

Instructions:

1. Cook pasta according to package instructions. Drain and set aside.
2. In a large bowl, mix cooked pasta, chicken, pesto, cherry tomatoes, salt, and pepper.
3. Serve with grated Parmesan on top.

Flan

Ingredients:

- 1 cup sugar (for caramel)
- 1 can (14 oz) sweetened condensed milk
- 1 can (12 oz) evaporated milk
- 3 eggs
- 1 tbsp vanilla extract

Instructions:

1. Preheat oven to 350°F (175°C). In a saucepan, melt sugar over medium heat until golden brown. Pour caramel into a flan mold or cake pan.
2. In a blender, combine condensed milk, evaporated milk, eggs, and vanilla. Blend until smooth.
3. Pour mixture over caramel in the pan. Place in a larger baking dish filled with water (water bath).
4. Bake for 50-60 minutes until set. Let cool, then refrigerate before inverting onto a plate to serve.

Enjoy these delightful recipes!

Milton Keynes UK
Ingram Content Group UK Ltd.
UKHW051316041024
2011UKWH00053B/235